Building Retirement Now

YOUR SECURED RETIREMENT BLUEPRINT™
FROM PLANNING AND DESIGN TO EXECUTION

Joseph S. Lucey, CFP®, RFC

Secured Retirement Financial
MINNEAPOLIS, MINNESOTA
www.securedretirements.com

Joseph S. Lucey/Secured Retirement Financial
5775 Wayzata Blvd, Ste 830
St. Louis Park, MN 55416
www.securedretirements.com

Book layout ©2013 BookDesignTemplates.com

Building Retirement Now/ Joseph S. Lucey. —1st ed.
ISBN 9781796222777

Disclosures

Contents

Foreword i

Chapter 1: Barb and Tom 1

Chapter 2: Lynn and Robert 17

Chapter 3: Lynn and Robert 2 33

Chapter 4: Marlene 43

Chapter 5: "Be Better Than You Are" 69

Chapter 6: Excellence Awaits You 77

About the Author 83

About Secured Retirement Financial 85

Contact 87

To my son, who makes all the work
for team Gavin-and-Dad worth it

Foreword

"The goal is to provide inspiring information that moves people to action." – Guy Kawasaki

People like you.

That's what this book is about. That's for whom it is written.

People like you are the reason, each and every morning, without fail, I feel blessed on my commute into the office of Secured Retirement Financial.

I had to travel a bumpy road to get to where I am today. Perhaps you have, too.

If you've had dealings with financial advisors, you likely have experienced the biggest pitfall of the financial services industry. It is thick with "big box" corporate brokerage firms and is the opposite of swift when it comes to delivering thoughtful, personalized service.

I think you know what I mean. I think we can all agree that it's better to treat people like actual human beings, rather than sales quotas.

I learned this lesson about a quarter-century ago. At the time, I was just starting my career, employed as a financial advisor at Prudential Securities (one of the "big box" firms). It didn't take me long to discover that my job didn't involve actual advising. Rather, it was selling the company's financial products to clients, all the while making sure I sold enough of them to make my manager's monthly sales goal.

No thanks.

Soon thereafter, I quit to start my own company. I believed there had to be a better way—the only way, for me—in which serving people's interests was job one instead of meeting corporate sales projections.

I founded Secured Retirement Financial on the premise that people come first. Everyone has a unique story and a unique situation. Because of this, every person, whether their retirement investment accounts hold $10,000 or $10 million, deserves to be treated with respect, honesty, and humanity by someone whose only fiduciary duty is to the client. Period.

At Secured Retirement Financial, this isn't a slogan or lip service, it's how we live and how we establish, maintain, and nurture relationships.

During the past two-plus decades and counting, Secured Retirement Financial has been privileged to collaborate with people just like you, serving as an advocate and partner in assisting, creating, and advising individuals and couples in retirement planning.

In the following chapters, it is my hope that you will learn something about Secured Retirement Financial and the relationships we attempt to build. In these narratives, you'll discover how a few of the relationships started and eventually bloomed.

While each client story is different, one axiom unites them. Each of our clients were unwilling to brave the retirement journey alone. They were determined to do it right. They decided to trust someone who provided personalized, thoughtful counsel, someone who treated them like an actual person, someone who first made their acquaintance by showing them that trust isn't given but earned.

After you're finished reading, it is my hope that you allow Secured Retirement Financial the opportunity to forge a relationship and earn your confidence.

Here's to the best days of your life. May they be better than you ever imagined.

Joe Lucey, CFP®, RFC
St. Louis Park, Minnesota

CHAPTER 1

Barb and Tom: A Love Story

Two things were obvious when Barb and Tom visited my office for the first time.

With forty-four years of marriage, three grown kids, and a second grandbaby on the way, they had spent a lot of time together. But you could tell that the couple was still very much in love. It was the little things that gave them away.

Barb and Tom held hands at every opportunity, which was what they were doing when they arrived for their appointment on a crisp and sunny spring morning. As we were about to begin our meeting, Tom made sure to pull out Barb's chair before she sat down. His "bride," as Tom usually called her, expressed her thanks toward him, not with words, but by showing him a sweet smile followed by a peck on her husband's cheek.

Yet, despite their obvious affection for each other, the second characteristic was also obvious. And it wasn't as sweet as their love.

You could tell that Tom didn't want to be there. As he settled into his seat next to his wife, the expression on his face said everything I needed to know: He would've preferred to be mowing the lawn in a hailstorm during a tornado warning instead of sitting in the office of a financial professional.

Tom's aversion to our meeting started our morning with a dull thud. With Barb and Tom already seated, I was about to assume my place across from them when Tom plopped down a stack of paperwork—retirement account statements, Social Security documents, legal papers, and more—on the conference room table.

"There's our stuff," Tom said curtly. "Have at it. I doubt you'll be able to do anything with it. I mean, anything that could help us that we're not already doing. You know our friend, Gloria, who referred us to you. She told you we already have a financial person and aren't looking for a new one, didn't she? But since my bride gave me no choice but to come with her to see you today, it's all yours to do something with it. I'm sure you'll find something one way or another."

ACCORDING TO CHARLES SCHWAB, NOTHING MUCH IS HAPPENING WHEN IT COMES TO PLANNING FOR RETIREMENT. IN FACT, ONLY ABOUT A FOURTH OF ALL AMERICANS HAVE A *WRITTEN* PLAN FOR RETIREMENT. THINK ABOUT THAT. NO LIFESTYLE PLAN, NO UNDERSTANDING OF INCOME, NO GOALS. NOTHING WRITTEN DOWN BY THE VAST MAJORITY OF AMERICANS.

CHARLES SCHWAB. JUNE 2017. "HOW AMERICANS DEFINE AND MANAGE THEIR WEALTH." HTTPS://ABOUTSCHWAB.COM/IM-AGES/UPLOADS/IN-LINE/CHARLES_SCHWAB-MODERN_WEALTH_INDEX-FIND-INGS_DECK.PDF.

I fully understood what Tom was trying to say. I can't say I blamed him for the sarcasm. Chances are, neither can you.

The retirement planning stuff can get terribly confusing and fast. Plenty of people who work in the sector are slow to offer explanations—that is, if they provide any answers at all. There's no shortage of financial advisors who come across as overzealous when it comes to signing you up for one of the products they can sell you, which, in turn, fetches them a commission.

I completely understand if you don't trust those characters.

And the sales methods are only one way to sour a client. But the harder part about getting someone to sign up is the fear factor. Retirement planning can involve the most discomforting conversations. These can include discussing the ramifications of a spouse dying, or the specter of household bankruptcy in the wake of unforeseen medical bills.

Scary? You betcha.

"Barb, Tom," I began. "First of all, I appreciate your time. I appreciate both of you coming here today. Second, just so you two understand where I'm coming from, there might not be a darn thing I can do for your retirement planning."

"Oh really?" said Tom sardonically. "That's hard to believe."

I continued. "If we get through all your "stuff," as you called it, Tom, and there's nothing that shows opportunities for how the two of you can better take back your retirement income, there's nothing I can point to that'll help you folks plan more efficiently. You might not have any holes in your plan or opportunities to get better peace of mind, additional income, or whatever it may be. If that's the case, then I'm going to say so up front because I don't want to waste your time, or frankly, my time, for that matter."

There was a pause, and then I went on.

"I'm here to find out if reason exists for us to have a relationship, to discover, one way or another, if you and your retirement plan will benefit from a partnership with me."

Barb went on to explain why the two of them were in my office that day. It was her who first instigated the meeting. Tom, not so much. He was very unlike his bride, who was immediately open to new information when it came to finance. She immediately signed up for attendence at the informational retirement planning event I'd hosted the previous week at a restaurant in northeast Minneapolis. But like I said, Tom wasn't feeling it this morning in early April.

"Joe, don't take this the wrong way," Tom said. "But we all know your certified financial whatcha-ma-call-it is just a glorified title for *salesman*. We know your job is to sell us on you, whether it's right for us or not. I mean, you don't get paid unless you're selling clients something, signing up somebody new, like us, for one of the financial products you represent."

I completely understand Tom's comment. After working as a CERTIFIED FINANCIAL PLANNER™ for almost a quarter of a century—not to mention my industry experience prior to certification—I can say it's not new to meet with apprehensive clients. Often, within a married couple, at least one member of the party feels bothered by the whole affair. But still, the thing I love the most is blunt candor. I welcome it with open arms, especially in the office.

Tom, Barb, and I were having an honest conversation, and we were making progress.

"Before we delve into the nuts and bolts of this stuff, answer this one question for me please," I told Barb and Tom. "Tell me, what it is you want all this financial stuff to do for the two of you? In other words, paint me a picture. What does retirement look like for the two of you?"

Barb and Tom looked at each other for a solid few seconds and said nothing. Barb was the one to break the silence.

"Give us a few minutes to think that over, would you, Joe?" Barb said. "That's a question nobody has ever asked us before."

"She's right," said Tom. "Why hasn't anyone ever asked us that?"

Throughout my relationship with Tom and Barb, starting the first day they walked into my office, I got to know their story.

Tom was sixty-seven years old and a Vietnam-era vet who did his service at a logistic base in Japan. He grew up on a farm in southeastern Iowa. Hogs and high school wrestling had taught him the meaning of hard work, and eventually the GI Bill greased the wheels for him to go to college. That's where he met Barb and the two of them fell in love.

Tom spent his entire career at a big construction contracting company that hired him straight out of college. He'd worked his way up to senior project manager. When he wasn't putting in long days on job sites, Tom would either be on the golf course or at his desk at home where he read the Wall Street Journal six days a week. Now, at his age, he enjoyed picking stocks via online trading from the comfort of the big leather chair that the kids had gotten him for his sixty-fifth birthday.

Barb, age sixty-four, handled the household bills and kept an eye on their retirement savings. She would celebrate her sixty-fifth birthday on July 4th. Marriage and children had delayed the start of her career in education, but after the couple's youngest child was out of the house, Barb went back to school, earning a degree in early childhood development. A career as a public-school teacher for special needs children followed. But circumstances in life caused Barb to retire early at age sixty-two. Her mom's health took a bad turn. She needed someone to help care for her and Barb took on that obligation.

"After Dad died, Mom really struggled," Barb would later tell me. "Almost all of what they'd been able to save for retirement was used to pay the medical bills when Dad got sick. The house was paid

> "BOTH THE PERCENTAGE OF OLDER AMERICANS CARRYING DEBT AND THE AMOUNT OF DEBT THEY'RE CARRYING ARE ON THE RISE. . . TODAY, 42% OF AMERICANS [AGE 56 TO 61] CARRY DEBT, AND WITH AN AVERAGE DEBT LOAD OF $17, 623."

NICK CLEMENTS. MARKETWATCH. SEPT. 28, 2017. "THIS IS SOMETHING RETIREES SHOULD BE WORRIED ABOUT." HTTPS://WWW.MARKETWATCH.COM/STORY/THE-BIG-THREAT-TO-RETIREMENT-DREAMS-2017-09-28

for, but all she had left was her Social Security. I don't think they ever thought to plan for a day like the one when Dad deteriorated like that."

Finally, all the years of Tom saving money by packing a lunch for work had finally paid off. By taking on more part-time tutoring jobs, Barb was able to earn a little extra income for the family.

Between their retirement accounts, the couple had amassed $1.2 million. While some neighbors had taken out hefty mortgages to move to supposedly sexier suburbs, Barb and Tom had remained in their longtime house in Bloomington where they had raised their kids. The home, valued around $350,000, would be paid off in eighteen months.

With Barb turning sixty-five in mid-summer, the couple's plan was to solely live off Social Security income, which amounted to $4,200 per month between the two of them.

"Ever since I can remember," Tom would say, "I was taught that you don't touch the money in your IRA when you finally retire. You leave that alone and just live off Social Security."

Their financial advisor had been the source of the advice. He also happened to be Tom's old college roommate. According to the quarterly IRA statements that arrived in the mail over the decades, he'd served the couple well.

But Tom's old friend himself was working toward his own retirement, which had come as surprise news. Barb had found out from a phone call a few months back. A stranger's voice introduced himself with a name she'd never heard of before. The young man on the other line had said how he was excited to be their new financial advisor.

The incident bothered Barb. In their household, she took responsibility for all the bills, balanced the checkbook, and kept tabs on the IRAs. But Barb happened to be good friends with one of my longtime clients, Gloria. Barb told Gloria about the unnerving call from someone claiming to be Barb's new advisor. Gloria suggested my name. Soon, Barb attended one of my events.

Barb first approached me that night after my presentation. Within two minutes, I could distinguish her motivating factor, what had brought her there. It wasn't that she was confused about retirement planning. She had no fear of partaking in squeamish conversations about health care expenses. But she did have love. For Tom. For their family. For the best days that lay ahead.

Barb, out of concern for herself and her family, wanted to feel empowered in retirement planning. She and Tom had given each other their best for all their years of marriage. Now, they were on the cusp of reaping the benefits of so much hard work and sacrifice. Barb had been searching for a retirement planner who understood. Someone who would honor the hard-working people they were and what they wanted around the corner come retirement.

She was looking for someone she and Tom could both trust.

Barb had faith that she would come into contact with someone like that, and she eventually found me. It was her faith that would convince to place their trust in me. And it is the faith of every single one of my clients that I hold sacred.

Every day, I work my hardest so that the people I am working with know and feel I'm doing this all for them. Making sure good people get to fully enjoy retirement makes us all happier people. That's why I feel blessed to do this job every day. That's why I created the comprehensive plan for a secured

WHAT ARE YOUR GOALS FOR RETIREMENT? TRAVEL? VOLUNTEERING AT CHURCH OR SCHOOL? SPENDING TIME WITH THE GRANDKIDS? HOBBIES? WHEN PLANNING YOUR RETIREMENT, DON'T LEAVE ANY STONE UNTURNED. WHEN YOU'RE CALCULATING YOUR FUNDS, YOU SHOULD CALCULATE HOW MUCH YOU ANTICIPATE SPENDING, RATHER THAN WHAT YOU THINK YOU CAN AFFORD TO SPEND. REMEMBER, YOU'RE WRITING UP A LIFESTYLE PLAN, AND YOU SHOULD CONSIDER EVERY POSSIBLE EXPENSE.

retirement that encompasses Social Security, personal retirement savings, tax planning, and health care.

And this is why I'd asked Barb and Tom the question I mentioned earlier: "What is it you want this stuff to do for the two of you?"

During our first meeting, the couple indicated the following: They were prepared to live solely off Social Security, about $50,000 annually, but they wished they had maybe $10,000 to $15,000 more per year. Their goal was to travel and help out the kids at

Christmas, if they needed a little boost. Rome and New Zealand topped the list of vacation destinations.

Barb and Tom had also chatted about one day maybe buying a condo down south. Friends had spoken glowingly of Mesa, Arizona. Leaving some inheritance for their kids appealed to the couple, but that wasn't a top priority. Instead, their biggest goal was to make their retirement income last until the end. Planning for the inevitable day that one of them would pass on was their most important priority.

The three of us hammered away at their financial stuff. We discovered they could use some income from their IRAs and defer drawing on their Social Security payouts. In other words, Barb and Tom could plan to live on $70,000 annually—$20,000 more than they had envisioned—by conservatively modifying their retirement plan.

"See here," I showed Tom and Barb, "by deferring a portion of your Social Security benefits over the next few years, you'll be in a better position tax-wise, because then you're going to need to take the required minimum distribution from your IRA. Otherwise, the consequences from Uncle Sam could be a 50 percent tax penalty."

All that might sound confusing, but that's what I'm here for. It's what all fiduciaries can help you with, if you feel lost within your overwhelming pile of statements and accounts. It was so satisfying for me to help Barb and Tom organize their funds. Experiences such as this are why I have so much passion for what I do. Retirement planning isn't simply putting money in a 401(k). It requires a much more comprehensive program.

That's what the three of us were working on: tax planning and income planning around Social Security so Barb and Tom could maximize their retirement income with peace of mind.

"You couldn't be more right," Tom affirmed once we laid out all their ducks in a row. "Hoarding our money doesn't do us much good. We don't want to be too busy worrying about the future. But we do want to be prepared for the time if, God forbid, something unforeseen like medical bills takes us out at the knees because we weren't smart and didn't plan for the road ahead."

You bet we were making progress.

When we all felt like we couldn't bump around their accounts any further, I leaned back in my chair and stretched. Barb and Tom talked quietly, yet excitedly, to each other. How the energy in the room had changed over the course of an hour! Things felt so much lighter, the couple's future noticeably more abundant with choices, possibilities, and knowledge.

"We came in here today with a bunch of seemingly meaningless papers," Barb said. "Now you're showing us how to organize it, how to put it into places so all of the different piles work together for us in retirement. I can't tell you how much better that makes me feel."

"That goes the same for me too," said Tom.

I couldn't help but smile. For me, this excitement is what my job is all about.

I leaned forward with forearms on the edge of the table, my fingers steepled and horizontal to the flat surface. I acknowledged Barb first, though what I was about to say was intended for both of them. Turning to her husband, I made certain there was direct eye contact and said: "Tom, what's your gut, your intuition telling you about what we're doing? Why are the three of us here? What do you think about what I do?"

"I think you have something really special going on here, in this office," Tom said with a smile.

So concluded my first meeting with Tom and Barb. It's hard to believe that was eight years ago.

Much more recently, on a summer day, just weeks after their family had celebrated another birthday for Barb, Tom sat across from my office desk, chuckling.

Every time we meet he likes to remind me of the first time we met.

ARE YOU CONFIDENT YOU HAVE YOUR FINANCES IN ORDER? A NORTHWESTERN MUTUAL STUDY SAYS "INDIVIDUALS WITHOUT AN ADVISOR ARE TWICE AS LIKELY AS PEOPLE WITH AN ADVISOR (34% VS 13%) TO SAY THEY ARE 'NOT AT ALL CONFIDENT' THEY HAVE THE BALANCE BETWEEN SPENDING AND SAVING." HAVING AN ADVISOR LOOKING OUT FOR YOUR NEEDS MIGHT BE THE NEXT STEP TO YOUR BEST RETIREMENT.

NORTHWESTERN MUTUAL. 2018. "PLANNING AND PROGRESS STUDY." HTTPS://NEWS.NORTHWESTERNMU-TUAL.COM/PLANNING-AND-PRO-GRESS-2018.

"You're lucky my bride thought you knew your stuff, otherwise she wouldn't have pushed me to spend an hour at your office with you," Tom said. "I couldn't have admitted it then, but I could tell you knew your stuff. Even so, I could've taken it or left it. There are, after all, plenty of smart people in the world."

We laughed at Tom's stubbornness, but then he went on.

"But remember the question you asked? You asked, 'What was it that you want this stuff to do for you?' That question was what really caught my attention. It made me start to think that there was something different going on here. That maybe I should listen to you, if you were going to take the time to listen to me."

I could not feel more blessed to know Barb and Tom, and their family.

I'll never forget the party for the couple's fiftieth wedding anniversary. Something like 150 people attended.

Tom's golf game has improved considerably the past five years thanks to wintering in Mesa, where the couple purchased their dream condo.

Barb is busier than ever, too. She's helping their second grandchild, Amy, prepare to leave for college. She was recently accepted to the Naval Academy in Annapolis, and she is due to report to Maryland come summer.

Back in my office, Tom reflected on life in general.

"Joe," he said, "The day we first met, I didn't want to be there. Now, look at us! I actually look forward to visiting you. I enjoy coming here and learning from the things you have to say. Who would have thought how one spring morning could've have done so much to change our lives?

I looked at Tom, saying nothing, allowing the smile on my face to say it all.

CHAPTER 2

Lynn and Robert, Part One

In high school, Lynn was an honor roll student. She sat first chair French horn in the high school band. She played point guard for the varsity basketball team where she was a fixture in the starting lineup since ninth grade.

Robert was another one of the 113 classmates at the rural high school. Unlike Lynn, extracurricular activities weren't his thing. Instead, it was studying. Before first bell and after lunch hour, there was Robert, settled in a corner all by his lonesome, with a book in his lap, wearing a satisfied smile, showing dimples that were to die for. Report cards would show not one grade below A-minus since ninth grade.

From the first day of freshmen year to graduation, Lynn, the all-American girl, and Robert, the smart loner boy, barely spoke a word. But fate had a plan.

Two years passed. Robert, an education major, was enrolled for summer session at the University of Minnesota. Lynn, majoring in botany at a tiny East Coast college, had returned home months earlier. Her grandfather, a successful farmer, was ill. Grandma needed help keeping things running, which is what Lynn did six days a week.

But late in the afternoon each Saturday, Lynn absconded to the Twin Cities. She spent those nights in her best friend's dorm room and slept on the couch. On Sunday morning, Lynn would work behind the counter at Dayton's in downtown Minneapolis. The retail shifts provided respite from the grind of the farm. During those days, Lynn had some extra income to boot.

One Sunday in July, around lunchtime, Lynn watched a young man making his way through the store. There was eye contact. When he smiled, Lynn beheld those dimples that were to die for.

Lynn and Robert shared their love story like it happened yesterday. And this year marks their thirty-eighth wedding anniversary.

With three kids all grown up and the youngest in college, an empty nest served as a daily reminder to Lynn and Robert that life was transitioning for the couple. As both approached age sixty, the empty-nesters often found themselves thinking about the next chapter they would write together.

In the dawning age of their retirement, the couple could not have been more excited. As they examined their future with feelings of promise and possibilities, they imagined resplendent visions of what was to come.

They had visions. Lynn had dreams of getting back to her roots and playing in the dirt. She wanted to perfect the art of gardening.

For Robert, his dream is tinkering in the garage, refurbishing the Massey Ferguson 135 tractor he inherited from his father-in-law.

For all the beauty they hoped to experience in their retirement tomorrows, there were also feelings of anxiousness and uncertainty. This was why the couple called Secured Retirement Financial and scheduled an appointment. They were motivated to get their retirement plan together after listening to my radio show.

In addition to serving as a CERTIFIED FINANCIAL PLANNER™ professional, Registered Financial Consultant, and founder and president of Secured Retirement Financial, I host "Secured Retirement Radio," airing Saturday mornings on Twin Cities News Talk AM1130.

During our first session, Lynn and Robert shared photos of their families on their cell phones. I also showed them photos of my family. After a few laughs and stories, I then listened as the couple explained the concerns they had about their existing retirement plan.

"We started planning for our retirement, thinking about it really hard in our early fifties," Robert said. "We eventually came up with a plan, a plan that spelled out where it would start, how much we would need, and what income we would live on once we stopped working.

"We heard you on the radio last month, and I remember you talked about how retirement planning is so much bigger than just investment returns. That's what initially caught my attention. It got me thinking, wondering if our retirement plan wasn't the good plan we thought it was after all. What if it was missing pieces we hadn't even thought of? What if it had holes?"

Lynn nodded in agreement and said, "Truth be told, Joe, we've both been unsure about our retirement plan for a while. Our apprehensions started when we had relatives and people we love dearly who retired. We saw them suffer after something happened that they weren't prepared for. Then what you were saying on the radio, that's what made us finally listen to our intuition. That's what brings us here."

Squaring my chair snuggly to the table, I told Lynn and Robert that I understood everything they were saying. I commended them for following their instincts. I told them how grateful I was for the opportunity to show them what a complete retirement plan looked like, and that I was excited for beginning the planning stage with them.

"There are two things I want to share right off the bat," I said to Robert and Lynn. "I can promise the discussion we will have here will go a long way to ease any of your uncomfortable feelings. The other thing is this: Worrying is like being in a rocking chair. It gives you something to do, but it doesn't really get you anywhere. Both of you can now give yourselves permission to stop worrying. You've already made the choice to be empowered in your retirement planning. Otherwise, you wouldn't be here. I don't hesitate for a moment when I say that good stuff is happening here today."

At the time the two of them visited me, Lynn was preparing to turn fifty-nine in the fall, and Robert recently celebrated his fifty-ninth birthday. Their eldest daughter Grace, was pursuing a Ph.D. at a university in the Netherlands and was married to another academic. The two of them were yet to have kids. Their youngest child, Zelly, was studying to be a veterinarian.

Lynn explained more about Zelly. She had wanted to be a vet since she was eleven years old. Lynn's father, now deceased, made his daughter and son-in-law promise him something during his last days. If Zelly one day showed the grit and wherewithal to get into veterinary school, Lynn and Robert had to do everything in their power to make it happen. Namely, they had to pay the tuition, which they knew wouldn't come cheap.

In their retirement plan, Lynn and Robert knew they had to factor in the cost of covering Zelly's tuition.

As for their middle child, George, he was married with two small kids, and worked as a teacher, the same profession as his father.

Then the couple began telling me about what they'd been doing with their lives up to that point.

Robert still worked as a career high school history and civics teacher. Lynn was primarily a stay-at-home mom but had worked part-time behind the cosmetics counter at a high-end department store. She spent time volunteering at a yarn shop that a friend owned. She also helped at events for Special Olympics.

The couple wanted to retire in about three years when both were sixty-two.

YOU MIGHT HAVE HEARD OF THE CONCEPT OF THE THREE-LEGGED STOOL BEFORE. BASICALLY, THE SEAT OF THE STOOL IS YOUR RETIREMENT INCOME, AND THE SEAT RESTS ON THREE LEGS. THE FIRST LEG IS SOCIAL SECURITY (A WOBBLY LEG GIVEN CURRENT PROJECTIONS OF THE GOVERNMENT PROGRAM'S BUDGET). THE SECOND IS THE PENSION PLAN, IF YOU HAVE ONE. THE THIRD LEG IS PERSONAL SAVINGS. WHICH LEGS ARE SUPPORTING YOUR RETIREMENT?

Their retirement investment accounts held $560,000. They inherited another $300,000 from Lynn's family. Robert's pension was to pay out about $2,500 monthly. Together, they were expecting $40,000 per year from Social Security. They owed about $50,000 on their home, valued at $350,000. They owned a rental duplex. It had $30,000 remaining on the note. The rental generated cash flow of $1,800 per month.

Upon retirement, Lynn and Robert hoped to sell their suburban home, then apply the proceeds to purchase a farmhouse with a bit of land within a ninety-mile radius of the Twin Cities. That's where

Lynn would have her big garden with flowers, herbs and vegetables. Robert envisioned a spacious garage where he would turn the refurbishment of the vintage tractor into one of life's crowning achievements.

After hearing the couple's many notable goals, I began pointing out the details of their retirement funds, helping them to see how they could take full advantage of them.

"Your plan of living off the rental income and taking Social Security, that might not be what works best in your situation," I told them. "I can see we need to take a hard look at not only how you're taking back your income in retirement, but also where it's coming from and when you're taking it."

When they said they had the same tax person for eighteen years and the same financial advisor for almost as long, I asked, "Has your financial advisor ever had a discussion with your tax person, or vice versa, about your retirement planning?"

The puzzled look on their faces told me the answer was no.

Like many of their generation, Baby Boomers born in the late fifties to mid-sixties, Lynn and Robert grew up in homes where parents preached blue-collar work ethic and to save, save, save for retirement. Boomers were told to sock money away regularly in an IRA. They were warned not to dare touch it.

According to the conventional wisdom that Robert and Lynn were taught, Social Security was the main source of income that paid for retirement. As for the money sitting in an IRA, maybe this was the time for them to realize that drawing from that account wouldn't be considered an act of sacrilege.

Maybe. Someday. Maybe.

Robert and Lynn were not alone in their struggle to figure out their next big financial step. In fact, I would argue they're part of the majority. Income greases the wheels of retirement. On that I hope we can all agree. Income rests on the entirety of retirement education for most Americans.

Therein lies the rub.

The income plan, in and of itself, isn't a retirement plan. It is a crucial component, but only one of the five elements that compose the comprehensive retirement planning from Secured Retirement Financial.

If you're like most people, nobody has ever told you there is a different, smarter way to tap into retirement income and plan for it to last a lifetime. At Secured Retirement Financial, we have the blueprint to potentially maximize what we call "Mailbox Income," which is simply steady payments that arrive each month. These kinds of funds include things like Social Security, pension, and annuity payouts.

HAVE YOU THOUGHT ABOUT TAPPING INTO YOUR RETIREMENT FUNDS BEFORE YOU ACTUALLY RETIRE? BEFORE YOU DO, CONSIDER THE MANY FEES, PENALTIES, AND/OR TAXES THAT YOU MIGHT HAVE TO PAY FOR IN ORDER TO RECEIVE THOSE FUNDS EARLY. IT'S IMPORTANT TO WORK WITH A FINANCIAL PROFESSIONAL WHO CAN HELP YOU EVALUATE YOUR SITUATION AND ACCESS YOUR INVESTMENTS WITH THE MOST EFFICIENT APPROACH.

On the road of retirement planning, the Income Roadmap™ by Secured Retirement Financial is a turn-by-turn directional guide on how to make your retirement income last a lifetime. It will show how you can best take back your retirement income. It will show you the income plan built with efficiency in mind. With efficiency comes returns that pay out over a lifetime.

Lynn, Robert, and I dug into their paperwork, our trio collaborating to craft an income plan, which would be a big part of their comprehensive retirement plan. By applying the Secured Retirement Financial Income Roadmap™, we examined the various retirement sources of income: a pension, Social Security, an IRA, and rental property. We discussed how much they needed to live on and the different ways it could be done.

Within a short time, we generated a working draft of the couple's income plan, a plan that combined their pension, Social Security, rental proceeds, and modest IRA draws.

I asked them about something Lynn mentioned earlier. She had said they had family members who suffered hardships in retirement. Lynn intimated the problems that stemmed from insufficient retirement planning.

"If it's not too much of an intrusion," I said, "I'd like to know more about that."

The plight of Robert's Aunt Bernice and her husband, Leo, offered a sad, yet cautionary tale about retirement planning.

"One day, Uncle Leo's forgetfulness got much worse," Robert said. "The next thing we all came to know is he had full-blown Alzheimer's disease and couldn't live on the farm anymore. He had to leave the only home he's ever known."

Both Leo and Aunt Bernice were in their mid-seventies when doctors first made the Alzheimer's diagnosis, he explained.

"Auntie didn't have a choice. She placed him in one of those intensive long-term care places where he lived until pneumonia got him," Robert continued. "He died without recognizing the face of the woman he'd been married to for half a century," said Robert. "For his care, at a cost of almost $95,000 a year, it didn't take that long for her to use up the entirety of their retirement investments.

"After he passed, she lost some of what they were receiving in their monthly Social Security. If that wasn't bad enough, I remember her talking about getting a big IRS tax bill the next year. She didn't get into the particulars. And I didn't ask because I could tell she was embarrassed about it."

Watching what happened to relatives jolted Lynn's system much like it did Robert's.

"I remember one day as this was happening," she said, "I turned to Robert and we stared at one another for a moment. It was me who said: 'What if something like that happened to us?'"

"For so long, neither of us had the answer," Robert says. "Neither of us knew to whom we should turn. Then that one Saturday morning, we heard you on the radio."

My heart sank after listening to the story about Bernice and Leo. I knew that much of their hardship could have been mitigated with better planning.

"There are some things in our life that we know we aren't able to control," Lynn said. "Like health issues, like what happened to Uncle Leo. But now, we do have a better understanding of the potential pitfalls for retirement-aged people."

She was right.

Does your current retirement plan include the what-ifs? What if one spouse falls sick and needs long-term care in a nursing facility? What if, and when, one of you passes away and the surviving spouse is faced with less retirement income and possibly higher tax bills?

DID YOU GAPE AT THE $95,000 AUNT BERNICE HAD TO PAY? THAT AMOUNT ISN'T UNHEARD OF IN THE LONG-TERM CARE WORLD. ACCORDING TO GENWORTH FINANCIAL, THE ANNUAL MEDIAN COST FOR LTC RANGES FROM $48,000-$100,375 PER YEAR. THINK ABOUT HOW MUCH YOU MIGHT PAY FOR THREE YEARS IN A NURSING HOME, WHICH IS THE AVERAGE LENGTH OF STAY.

GENWORTH FINANCIAL. JUNE 2018. "HOW MUCH COULD LONG TERM CARE INSURANCE COST? HTTPS://WWW.GEN-WORTH.COM/PRODUCTS/CARE-FUNDING/LONG-TERM-CARE-INSUR-ANCE/LTC-INSURANCE-CALCULA-TOR.HTML.

Lynn and Robert's original retirement plan didn't account for such variables.

In due time, though, I would assist Lynn and Robert, and they would possess a comprehensive retirement plan. They would be well prepared for any scenario. With their plan, they would be positioned to fully enjoy the years ahead. The couple would soon enough take ownership of a retirement plan that had them covered.

At Secured Retirement Financial, this is what we do.

Robert and Lynn were feeling it. They were shown some of the differences between the retirement planning old hat versus the way that Secured Retirement Financial does retirement planning.

"Everything you've said here this morning, Joe, has really resonated," Robert said. "It's exactly the kind of information we've been missing. In this moment, I can honestly say I'm feeling so much better about our retirement planning than I was when I woke up this morning."

"I couldn't agree more," Lynn added. "What we had before and what we're putting together now with you is like night and day."

We had made good progress on the income plan. Lynn and Robert also possessed an awareness about the what-if scenarios included as part of their comprehensive retirement plan.

"What a great start we've had today," I said to them. "We've made real progress in creating a plan that takes care of the both of you just as well as you've taken care of each another for all these years. I'm excited and honored to be putting in this work with the both of you, to be starting a relationship that'll serve your family for years—no, make that decades—to come."

We wrapped up that first session. The air in the room felt light, optimistic. Outside, through the large conference room windows, we beheld sunshine touching everything in sight.

We all shook hands at the door, and I told the couple how happy it

MANY ADVISORS ARE STUCK IN RETIREMENT PLANNING OF THE PAST. THEY ARE UNWILLING TO RESEARCH CURRENT TRENDS AND INSTEAD ARE GIVING THE SAME ADVICE THEY DID TEN YEARS AGO. BUT, WITH ONLY 14 PERCENT OF EMPLOYERS OFFERING 401(K)-STYLE PLANS TO EMPLOYEES (AND EVEN FEWER OFFERING PENSIONS), OLDER STRATEGIES FOR RETIREMENT INCOME JUST WON'T WORK.

CNBC. NOV. 1, 2017. "TRADITIONAL RETIREMENT IS DEAD." HTTPS://WWW.CNBC.COM/2017/11/01/TRADITIONAL-RETIREMENT-IS-DEAD.HTML

made me to know that they're feeling positive about their future. Before the couple walked out, I told them that the best part might still be yet to come.

Lynn and Robert continued to schedule appointments, and we had many healthy discussions about the couple's retirement future.

CHAPTER 3

Lynn and Robert, Part Two

The following week, Lynn and Robert returned to Secured Retirement Financial for their second meeting. They arrived at the office with ideas, questions, and positive energy. From the moment they walked in, I could tell they were already feeling the gifts of transformation.

Taxes were the big subject during the second meeting. It might sound like a drab topic to most people, but a retirement plan calls for thoughtful, proper tax planning that can achieve *epic* results.

I found myself explaining this to Lynn and Robert as we stood in the elevator, headed toward my office.

I asked, "Did either of you know that in retirement, some families will pay next to no taxes on Social Security while other families will pay through the nose? It all depends on how you plan and when to choose to take it back.

The elevator dinged. The doors opened. The couple stepped forward. Something stopped Robert in his tracks. He turned around and looked me straight in the eye.

"Joe, I have a quick question," he said. "Why is it that nobody has ever asked us questions like these before?"

I smiled and explained that this world is bursting full of financial advisors. There are many that will only think of a client as a number, many that care more about their money than the actual person sitting across from them at their desk. But there are some firms like Secured Retirement Financial that have retirement planning vehicles geared toward changing lives. A key piece is involvement—both yours and ours—in the transformational retirement planning process.

The three of us settled into our chairs to begin the session. We got right to work.

"Last week was a great start, really good stuff," I said. "You guys came in, willing and ready with a vision about what you wanted your income to do in retirement. You have a good idea of what you want your life to look like as a couple. You know your goals. It made for a smooth transition into drafting an income plan."

Lynn and Robert began what we call the Income Roadmap™, and the first pillar of the Secured Retirement Blueprint™, a design for a successful retirement plan.

"As we continue to follow the roadmap, we arrive at the place with an ugly name, but I can promise you it can be beautiful: *taxes*."

I explained that the powers of transformation can't be unlocked without an understanding of relationships, the connective workings of different parts functioning as one. For the retirement plan to be optimal, or more specifically, to function most optimally, it has to be engineered to perform with efficiency.

For us at Secured Retirement Financial, that efficiency comes with careful consideration of every detail, including the ever-dreaded taxes.

> TAXES CAN BE A BIT UNPREDICTABLE IF YOU DON'T HAVE A PLAN. ONE STUDY SHOWED TAXES COULD FLUCTUATE BETWEEN AN EFFECTIVE TAX RATE OF ZERO AND NEARLY 30 PERCENT—THAT'S A PRETTY BIG DIFFERENCE.
>
> KATHLEEN COXWELL. NEW RETIREMENT. DEC. 28, 2017. "TAXES IN RETIREMENT."
> HTTPS://WWW.NEWRETIREMENT.COM/RETIREMENT/TAXES-IN-RETIREMENT-SHOULD-YOU-WORRY/

"Without tax planning as part of retirement planning," I told Robert and Lynn, "it's impossible for the plan to be comprehensive. I can't emphasize enough what a huge piece this is. In retirement, it's not what you get, but what you get to keep that counts most."

The two of them sat there, waiting for me to say more.

"Let me put it like this: As a rule, Americans plan for retirement by saving as much as they can during their working years. But as we approach the age when we stop working, the mindset shifts. How much money is there for retirement? How much income can we expect to get every month? How do we plan so we don't run out of money when we're retired? But here's the thing: Rarely, if ever, does anyone talk about efficiency in taking income, especially since we all know we're going to have to pay taxes."

Continuing, I added, "Sometimes I joke that in our accumulation years, it's all about ROI, 'Return On Investment.' But later, in retirement, ROI changes its meaning to 'Reliability Of Income.'"

Robert motioned to politely interrupt.

"I have two questions," He said. "Could you please define efficiency in more detail? Also, if we are understanding you correctly, are you saying there are ways to keep or lose income in retirement?"

I explained by saying that in retirement, efficiency has to do with taking back income from the accounts you were previously saving money. But taking back that income comes with new questions: What sources will give you those returns? How much can you attain? When can you get it? If your retirement plan discusses how much you'll have per month, and for how many years, it is incomplete. If your plan doesn't consider and involve tax implications along the way, you could be setting up someone in your family—whether it be yourself, or you and your spouse, or just your spouse—for rough, stressful days in the future.

Throughout this meeting, I asked Robert and Lynn a few questions about taxes.

THE MAJORITY OF AMERICANS BEGIN COLLECTING SOCIAL SECURITY AT THE YOUNGEST AGE AVAILABLE—SIXTY-TWO, DESPITE THE POTENTIAL FOR A HIGHER MONTHLY CHECK AND THE POTENTIAL TO RECEIVE MORE BENEFITS OVER A LIFESPAN.

HTTP://CRR.BC.EDU/BRIEFS/TRENDS-IN-SOCIAL-SECURITY-CLAIMING/

- Did you know a single filer pays much more in taxes than a couple filing jointly?
- Did you know a sixty-six-year-old retiree who postpones taking Social Security until age seventy could see their monthly payout increase by 32 percent?
- Did you know drawing from an IRA in lieu of Social Security for a few years not only yields more retirement income, but also drastically lightens tax liabilities in the coming years?

When I posed each of these questions to Lynn and Robert, both shook their heads no.

"Until now," I began, "there hasn't been a whole lot for the two of you as a working couple for opportunities that relate to tax planning. But what excites me is that, by transitioning into retirement, you are in control of so much more of where your income is going to come from. And by being in control, we're given so much more power over how we're going to be paying taxes. And, guys, I'm not talking about taxes for this year. I'm talking about paying taxes for the rest of your lives."

Robert and Lynn seemed relieved by the idea of fewer taxes.

Consider the tax plan component as a new way of thinking in the retirement planning process by

Secured Retirement Financial. We recognize its significance because retirement is different than any other time in your life when it comes to paying taxes.

For decades, you've earned. Twice a month or every two weeks, you received a paycheck. When we're working, the goal is earning. Yet, in doing so, we lose most of our ability to control how much we pay in taxes. Yes, based on your particular life circumstances, you may have one more deduction here or another there, but overall, we're more concerned with earning the most we can. Then we pay the tax bill commiserate with those earnings. But when we stop working, the big question becomes this: How do we replace those paychecks in the most tax-efficient manner possible?

The answer can allow us greater control over our overall payments.

For most people, retirement presents the first time in life to exert some degree of control on the amount of taxes they will pay. Since you get to choose how to take back income, you're also afforded choices about how much money Uncle Sam will get from you, and when the federal government will get it.

It seems like a no-brainer, doesn't it?

The government either gets more of your money when you're retired, or you get to plan to be stingy.

PUTTING OFF TAKING SOCIAL SECURITY COULD ADD AS MUCH AS 8 PERCENT PER YEAR TO YOUR MONTHLY CHECK UP TO AGE SEVENTY, MAKING DEFERRAL A NO-BRAINER FOR SOME COUPLES. BUT, WATCH OUT! THERE'S A LOT MORE TO THINK ABOUT THAN JUST GETTING THE BIGGEST CHECK. CONSIDER TAXES, YOUR HEALTH, AND THE EFFECT ON A SPOUSE'S SOCIAL SECURITY CHECK.

It makes you wonder why so many retirement plans don't take taxes into account.

Our collaborative hard work was bearing fruit, as Lynn and Robert's income plan had taken shape.

Using the Income Roadmap™, they were able to decide where to take money from first and how to make sure it would last a lifetime. Next, I offered some suggestions for changes to the income plan, a plan that's a combination of pension, Social Security, rental proceeds, and modest IRA draws. Everything was based on tax considerations. I showed them different choices, laying out the various pathways in taking back their retirement income, including the deferral of some Social Security benefits.

From there, they thought aloud by talking out various considerations.

We kept tweaking the income plan.

They really liked the modifications. You couldn't blame them. The plan, as we together engineered it, would provide them $15,000 per year more in income than they had anticipated. At the same time, it set them up for paying less in taxes for many years to come.

Robert and Lynn appeared to be a bit overwhelmed—in a good way.

"Incorporating tax planning as part of our overall retirement plan has exposed us to a whole new universe," Lynn said. "We

WHEN YOU'RE DECIDING WHETHER TO RELY FIRST ON SOCIAL SECURITY OR ASSETS FROM A RETIREMENT ACCOUNT LIKE AN IRA, YOU HAVE TO REMEMBER THAT SOCIAL SECURITY CAN'T BE PASSED ON TO THE NEXT GENERATION. THAT'S WHY IT'S SO IMPORTANT TO WORK WITH A FINANCIAL PROFESSIONAL AND TAKE A COMPREHENSIVE LOOK AT HOW SOCIAL SECURITY WILL WORK WITH YOUR INCOME PLAN.

had no idea. What we've been doing here with you Joe, I mean, this is planning at an entirely different level."

"Joe, I must admit," interjected Robert, "I was a little suspicious last week when you said the tax component could have the biggest impact on our retirement plan. 'Epic,' I think, is the word you used. But you were right. Now that you've shown us, we can see how it works in conjunction with the income plan. It's obvious how much of a difference it's going to make."

The couple was well on the way to ownership of a comprehensive Secured Retirement Blueprint™, a design for a successful retirement plan.

Welcome to the transformational approach in retirement planning.

Welcome to Secured Retirement Financial.

CHAPTER 4

Marlene: A New Day Rising

O h, thank you," Marlene said, taking the box of tissues from my hand.

She wiped the tears streaking her face. She took a few seconds to compose herself. Marlene's face rose to meet mine, her gaze a laser beam of melancholy directed toward where I sat across the conference room table. I let her cry things out.

"Before coming to your office today," said Marlene, attempting to catch her breath, "I told myself— I told myself that—that I was going to hold it together."

She continued wiping the tears away.

"But look at me," she continued. "We haven't even started the conversation, and I'm already a total wreck. You can't imagine how I dread talking about this stuff."

More tears flowed. They rolled over Marlene's cheekbones and past her chin, staining her emerald-green blouse.

"Take all the time you need, please," I said.

I gently reminded her that I was there for her. That everyone at Secured Retirement Financial was there for her.

"This conversation, today's meeting, it's all about seeing what we may do to improve your situation," I continued. "Please remember we have all the time in the world for you, if that's best for you."

As I finished my sentence, one of our team members from Secured Retirement Financial appeared in the doorway. With an empathetic smile, she offered Marlene a cup of green ginger tea.

"Thank you, dear," Marlene said. "That's very sweet of you. You must have been reading my mind. A cup of hot tea is exactly what I need at this moment."

Marlene took two easy sips. Slowly, her breathing returned to a balanced rhythm. Her tears retreated. She forced a slight smile.

Within moments, I could feel her embarrassment evaporating. Marlene's posture straightened. For a minute or two, neither of us said a word as I watched the heaviness in her countenance getting lighter and lighter.

On a partly sunny spring day, with dogwoods and daffodils perfuming the air, and the lakes around the Twin Cities populated by goslings, ducklings, and their protective parents, I was about to find out the reasons behind Marlene's sorrow.

"There are two things you should know about me, Joe," Marlene began. "First, I'm scared. In fact, I don't think I've ever felt this afraid since I lost my husband. And second: I don't trust people. I don't even trust you. I know nothing about you, your company, what you do, etcetera. No offense."

"None taken," I said. "Trust is too important for any of us to do it with blinders on. But I do hope that you give me—us—the opportunity to earn your trust. That's what today is all about. Trust starts with a conversation."

And a conversation is what happened over the next fifteen minutes, talking about anything and everything other than retirement and financial stuff.

She asked about me. My life. My history. My world.

I told her about my joining the U.S. Marines after high school, earning my bachelor's degree, and starting my own financial advisory firm after spending a few years working for other companies in the sector.

IS YOUR ADVISOR A FIDUCIARY? FINANCIAL ADVISORS CAN BE MANY THINGS, BUT THE MOST IMPORTANT TRAIT YOU NEED THEM TO HAVE IS FIDUCIARY STATUS. THESE FOLKS ARE LEGALLY REQUIRED TO ACT IN YOUR BEST INTEREST WHEN IT COMES TO HANDLING, INVESTING, AND ALLOCATING YOUR MONEY.

"Why did you go out on your own?" Marlene asked.

"Because I believe that to do this job right, to truly be in the business of serving people, it has to start with the heart," I said. "When I realized I couldn't do that working in this industry for somebody else, I made the decision and started Secured Retirement Financial."

By the look on her face, I could tell Marlene only half-way understood my answer.

"What I mean by that," I explained, "is I didn't want to be the kind of financial advisor whose job was to sell clients financial products X, Y, and Z because that's what made my employer money and he's the one who pays me commission. I wanted to work this industry differently. That's why I began a company founded on building relationships and serving people's best interests. In other words, I started a company that's built on the foundation of trust."

Marlene nodded, then said, "I like that answer."

She kept asking about my life, and I next told her about my family, wife Patty, and our son Gavin. I pulled out a few pictures I had of them and she admired them.

"But enough about me," I said. "Let's talk you. Give me some background about what it is that brings you here to see us, if you would, please."

At that time, Marlene was seventy-three years old and widowed. She'd traveled a circuitous path to arrive at Secured Retirement Financial.

"I should have first come to see you—gosh, has it really been almost twenty years ago now? —when my husband Curtis had just passed away," she said. "All that happened around the year 2002 or 2003, you know, during that period after 9/11 when everybody's investments were going down."

What stopped her from coming to see me then? Ironically, I came to find out it was trust, the very same thing that Marlene told me was just about dead inside her.

"In both cases," said Marlene, "I didn't come to you because I trusted what my financial person was telling me and continued to trust him despite feeling something inside of me that just didn't sit right. In

MARLENE IS UNFORTUNATELY NOT AN ISOLATED EXAMPLE OF WHAT HAPPENS WITH MANY WIDOWS. THE REALITY IS THAT MOST MEN DIE MARRIED AND MOST WOMEN DIE SINGLE—WOMEN TYPICALLY OUTLIVE THEIR HUSBANDS. THIS IS ONE REASON THAT, NO MATTER WHO IS THE FINANCIAL "ALPHA" OF THE RELATIONSHIP, SPOUSES MUST COMMUNICATE ABOUT THEIR FINANCIAL POSITIONS AND STRATEGIES ACROSS THE BOARD.

AMERICAN ASSOCIATION FOR LONG-TERM CARE INSURANCE. 2018. "LONG TERM CARE – IMPORTANT INFORMATION FOR WOMEN. HTTP://WWW.AALTCI.ORG/LONG-TERM-CARE-INSURANCE/LEARNING-CENTER/FOR-WOMEN.PHP

both instances, I trusted them to a fault because I so wanted to turn a blind eye to the problems happening around me."

She paused, wearing an expression that said Marlene was internally scarred from the experiences of history.

"To be fair, I had a hand in it. I was the enabler," continued Marlene. "I enabled things because it felt yucky, or dishonorable. That's probably a better word for it. I thought that I'd be a disrespectful wife if I didn't stay the course with what Curtis had spelled out for me to do with our retirement savings."

Marlene couldn't have been more wrong about one thing.

"You called yourself, the 'enabler,'" I said. "But from what I'm hearing, it sounds more like you were a wife who loved her husband."

A small smile graced her face. Marlene liked my version better, but you could tell she didn't believe it.

"Yeah, right, the loving wife," she said sarcastically. Anyone who saw her could tell she bore the burden of the loss of her husband. But it was also obvious that something else was weighing on her mind.

"'Mar-Mar,' was the nickname Curtis called me. 'Mar-Mar, do what I'm telling you and everything will turn out fine,' he told me."

For Marlene's sake, I wished things had played out the way Curtis envisioned. But they hadn't. Which is why Marlene recently had heeded the advice of her closest girlfriend by scheduling this appointment.

The retired couple who referred Marlene had been consulting with Secured Retirement Financial for less than two years. They initially came to us with an existing retirement plan in need of recalibration. But over the course of a few one-hour meetings, we had collaborated to rework various aspects of their retirement plan that needed refurbishing.

"What my friends said to me was that because of what the people at Secured Retirement had done for them, they felt as if a meeting with you would be beneficial for me, too," Marlene explained to me. "They also said you were good people."

Marlene eventually was able to wipe her tears away and tell me her story.

She and Curtis grew up on the Iron Range. Both were born into big families, five and seven kids, respectively, in which their fathers worked in the mining industry and their moms stayed at home. Marlene's dad worked as a heavy equipment operator at a mine near Mount Iron. The same mine employed Curtis' father as a mechanic.

Throughout Marlene's childhood, Christmas presents meant Santa brought each kid exactly one gift per year. At the home where Curtis grew up, Mom and Dad slept in the biggest bedroom. Meanwhile, the family's two daughters got the smaller one. As for the remaining five siblings—Curtis and four brothers—there was the living room. They slept four abreast on a pullout couch. The odd brother out got a sleeping bag on the floor.

"Poor as church mice, both of our families were," said Marlene. "But we wouldn't have wanted it any other way. Our childhoods were wonderful. I have only good memories."

By the end of their first year of middle school, Marlene and Curtis were sweethearts. They married the summer after high school graduation. By age nineteen, Marlene was pregnant. Curtis was a private in the United States Army.

With the mining industry in a freefall and the rest of the economy in northern Minnesota going down with it, Curtis decided to volunteer for the service. Shortly after boot camp, Marlene's young husband was in an airplane bound for Southeast Asia.

"Since we were both, I'd say fourteen or fifteen years old, Curtis and I had spoken about wanting to go to college," Marlene said. "We were both raised to believe that education was the way out of the mines and the way to better lives.

"Right about the time I got pregnant, Curtis told me he had a plan. He was going to enlist and after he'd served his time, we'd move somewhere good where we would make a life together."

Fortune would favor the young couple. The Vietnam War spared Curtis. When his tour as a combat soldier was over, the Army assigned him to a desk job stateside. Within a month of his discharge, Curtis packed everything the family owned in the back of a rusting '65 Chevy Nova. His wife and little girl in the passenger seat, and him at the wheel, heading south.

Their first home was a cramped apartment in Dinkytown, a neighborhood next to the University of Minnesota campus in Minneapolis. The apartment didn't even have its own bathroom. It shared one with the building's six other tenants.

Between studying for a class load that had him scheduled to earn a degree in less than four years, Curtis waited tables. Back on the home front, Marlene's plate was full as well, caring for their young daughter and working part-time as a receptionist at a local health clinic. Soon, she would be carrying a second child.

Their teamwork carried the young family to higher elevations. Using the GI Bill to pay for college, the couple squirreled away as much of Curtis' tips and Marlene's paychecks as they could.

Curtis did end up graduating early, like they wanted. On the same day of the commencement ceremony, he and Marlene put a down payment on a house. Shortly thereafter, Curtis began his career, working in the purchasing department at a start-up medical device firm.

The grand plan, which Curtis had conceived way back when, would continue to go according to script. Blessings started at home with the arrival of a third daughter. Marlene and their children came to the office where Curtis was putting in ten-hour days. He began receiving promotions. Heavier paychecks. Perks like an all-expenses-paid trip for Curtis and his wife to attend a six-day conference in Paris.

The daughters grew up fast. Too fast. Once they were old enough, Marlene enrolled at the University of Minnesota where she earned a nursing degree.

Marlene worked as a registered nurse for a few years before the Veterans Administration tapped her for a position where she supervised a staff of fifty.

There was one more huge change in their lives, perhaps one of the biggest and most heartbreaking of them all, which Marlene would remain unaware of until one day far off in the future. It would floor the unsuspecting wife and mother.

In late 1999, Curtis was diagnosed with pancreatic cancer. The bomb dropped the same day the couple's eldest child, Melissa, and her longtime boyfriend Jason announced they were engaged.

Into the New Year, Marlene's days were monopolized by working, wedding planning, and accompanying her husband to the oncology clinic. Into the spring, with Melissa's wedding plans made and Curtis' chemo and radiation sessions in the rearview, he and Marlene often found themselves on the front porch of their home in White Bear Lake. They'd talk about everything. About being kids on the Range. About funny memories with the girls. About the future, not theirs, but their girls', as in speculation about how many grandbabies they'd have, and which daughter would get married next.

THE AVERAGE REST-OF-LIFETIME SPENDING OF A RETIREE OVER SEVENTY IS AROUND $122,000 FOR HEALTH CARE ALONE—NOT INCLUDING THE COST OF LONG-TERM CARE. THINK ABOUT THAT AS DOUBLED FOR A COUPLE.

JOHN BAILEY JONES, ET AL. THE NATIONAL BUREAU OF ECONOMIC RESEARCH. JULY 2018. "THE LIFETIME MEDICAL SPENDING OF RETIREES." HTTPS://WWW.NBER.ORG/PAPERS/W24599.

As for what was to come for their retirement years, Marlene and Curtis left the topic of discussion unspoken, though they knew Curtis' health could deteriorate again.

The closest they came to discussing money happened on an evening during summer's swan song. It was an idyllic late August night in Minnesota, clear skies, no humidity, plenty of warmth, no mosquitoes. It was the Monday before the weekend their daughter was to be married. Snuggled on the porch sofa together, Curtis said there was something important he needed to tell Marlene about, something that most likely would surprise her, in a good way.

"He asked me if I remembered the retirement savings account he had set up, gosh, at that time, it was way back when, with his financial advisor, the guy he had gone to college with," Marlene said. "I said I did remember and, his name was 'Jim' something or another."

"Yes, Jim," Curtis said, impressed.

"And Jim has done good work for us," he continued, producing a little piece of paper from the pocket of his sweatpants, with a number scribbled on it. "The investments in our retirement nest egg add up to this number here."

Curtis handed it to her. Marlene couldn't believe it. The couple's nest egg now stood in the high six figures.

"And the last time I spoke with Jim, maybe two weeks ago," Curtis said to her, "he told me he thinks, that rather sooner than later, it'll have grown to more than a million."

Marlene didn't know what to say, staring at Curtis. She felt heartbroken, grateful, and crestfallen all at the same time. Curtis smiled. He too was speechless. They both cried, each silently resigned to an impending future that neither of them wanted. In the throes of that moment, Curtis asked his wife to promise him three things.

Marlene remembered. "He said, 'Work with Jim, my financial guy, and have him devise an investment strategy that first and foremost is designed to preserve the principal.'"

Secondly, Curtis said, make sure the investment plan includes a growth component, not risky, but moderate and lower, the idea being modest appreciations without the liabilities of losing the nest egg.

"The last thing he made me promise," said Marlene, "and this is where it gets really hard for me to talk about, was that . . . was that I was to use some of the money to pay for the girls' weddings and to help with their college, as best I could."

Curtis passed away at home five weeks after Melissa and Jason exchanged vows. Following Curtis's memorial service, Marlene had planned to take three weeks off from work. She didn't last one of those weeks, incapable of being in the quiet house, not knowing what to do with herself, alone.

Days became months, months became years. Marlene kept working, ten- to eleven-hour days becoming the norm. By age fifty-nine, she'd had enough. Greasing the wheels of her decision to quit working was the federal government's early retirement, a retirement that would see Marlene hit the ground running.

Trips to Spain, Croatia, and South Africa with girlfriends were early highlights. So was babysitting grandchildren. Some infrequent days, Marlene found herself earning a handsome wage, doing piecework as a consultant to hospitals and local health insurance companies.

Meanwhile, Marlene was continuing the relationship with Curtis' financial advisor just as she'd promised. She kept her word into the post-9/11 downturn. The advisor, Jim, calmed her worries with talk of staying the course and better days ahead. By mid-2003, the nest egg was breaking its shell.

"I'll never forget the day I got a call from him," she said. "He was saying how sorry he was that 40 percent of the principal was now gone. But after he had said that a dozen times, in thirteen different ways, he then said the good news is he had been working on a new investment plan for me, how its design was to reclaim what was lost, how I should schedule an appointment with his office, so he could tell me more in-person."

The face-to-face didn't happen. Instead, Marlene paid a visit to another financial advisor's office. Within forty-eight hours of Jim's phone call, Marlene sat in an unfamiliar office, listening to a different person explaining how confident he felt about his ideas to resurrect her retirement portfolio.

"My son-in-law recommended him," she said. "But I should have known better, right then and there, because I noticed that the new guy spoke the same language as the advisor I was leaving. But I reasoned that if I just trusted him, then everything was going to work out fine."

To a person she'd known for seventy-five minutes, Marlene turned over what was left of the nest egg.

Within six months, Marlene dipped into her retirement savings, despite her most recent financial statement, which didn't look good. The principal had lost half its value since Curtis had passed. Still, Marlene knew she didn't have a choice.

Daughter number two, Katie, was engaged. She and the future son-in-law, Rick, set a date. Marlene kept her worries to herself as the wedding plans took shape, watching retirement savings spent away on everything from booking one of the hottest bands in the Midwest to round-trip airfare and hotel for six of Rick's close relatives from South America, who couldn't afford to attend the event, but also couldn't afford not to attend, so said Rick, seconded by Katie.

The calendar flipped. The advent of springtime meant the date of the nuptials would soon be upon them. Despite the arrival of agreeable temperatures and blooming violets, Marlene had grown tired of her latest financial advisor.

"If the portfolio steadily losing money wasn't enough, I would get these calls from him on a pretty regular basis," Marlene said. "He would always be trying to get me to buy this new kind of mutual fund or that kind of annuity or some other kind of financial product.

"I can't tell you how many times that I told him I didn't need his latest financial product. What I needed was a more diversified plan. He told me I was already well-positioned, that I should expect things to rebound in the not-so-distant future."

As I sat at the table inside Secured Retirement Financial's meeting room, listening to Marlene pour out her

MORE THAN 70 PERCENT OF WIDOWS LEAVE THEIR ADVISOR AFTER THE DEATH OF THEIR SPOUSE. OFTEN, IT'S BECAUSE EVEN IF THE COUPLE WORKED WITH THE ADVISOR FOR DECADES, THEY DIDN'T EVER TAKE THE TIME TO DEVELOP A FULL RELATIONSHIP WITH THE WIDOW, OR TO BE SURE SHE UNDERSTOOD AND APPROVED OF THE FINANCIAL PLANS.

KATHLEEN REHL. INVESTMENT-NEWS. MAY 15, 2015. "HOW TO TALK TO WIDOWS AFTER THE DEATH OF A SPOUSE." HTTPS://WWW.INVESTMENT-NEWS.COM/ARTI-CLE/20150515/BLOG09/150519934 /HOW-TO-TALK-TO-CLIENTS-WHO-HAVE-JUST-BEEN-WIDOWED.

emotions to me, it was impossible not to feel for her. I could sense how she carried this overwhelming feeling that, somehow, she'd failed her husband.

The sound of silence filled the room, but Marlene's tears returned. They quickly were cascading down her face. The quiet was broken as her crying became uncontrollably audible.

Through the tears and shortness of breath, Marlene said: "What Curtis left me to protect, that which I promised him, is worth about thirty-five percent of what he left. I cannot even begin to tell you how that makes me feel."

Things bottomed out about two months ago, Marlene added. Her youngest daughter Heather had returned from studying abroad in Germany with a young man she announced was her fiancé.

"I know this is going to be the most expensive of the three weddings by far," said Marlene. "Heather has always said she wanted a big wedding and she's wanted it at this certain country club that costs as much as a new Honda. I do know that after this wedding, what Curtis left behind will be—"

At that moment, I said we should take a break. A Secured Retirement Financial employee asked Marlene if she'd like to go get a coffee at Caribou. Over the next twenty minutes, with Marlene away, I stayed in the conference room, writing down thoughts and ideas.

Marlene returned. We eased back into the conversation. She gushed, sharing with me her cellphone photos of her granddaughters, one an excellent swimmer, reputed to post some of the fastest times in the backstroke in the country for her age group. Another younger grandchild was equally gifted in a different craft; she was a cellist, chosen to attend a summer symposium at The Julliard School in New York City.

"I understand your anxieties about your retirement," I said after we got the conversation back to her retirement plan. "Three daughters, all of whom you've helped through college, at the same time, paying for all of their wedding expenses. You've done amazing."

That got a small smile out of Marlene.

"I hope that despite what we're talking about today, you remember to feel good, to feel proud about the love you've shared and happiness you've created. I'm sure Curtis, right now, wears a giant smile and is looking down on you."

She sipped her coffee between swatting tears. She gazed out the window at a May morning bladed by sunshine.

"If I may," I said, "I'd like to share with you a story about my son. It's a story about me learning a valuable lesson. It's about changing perspectives. I believe you'll appreciate it because I think we will be able to apply the same tenet to your situation."

Marlene nodded in affirmation.

I explained that Gavin arrived woefully premature. If Patty's pregnancy wasn't hard enough, Gavin's birth was exceptionally challenging.

He was born eight weeks premature. Gavin weighed as much as a bag of sugar. For the first six weeks of his life, I said to Marlene, our routine was back and forth to the neonatal intensive care unit, where we kept a vigil as nurses provided Gavin oxygen and administered a Bili light to treat his jaundice.

"The experience changed me and my perspective," I said. "It was this moment when some invisible power in the universe knocked me upside the head. Looking back at it now, I know I felt that way because during the early period of pregnancy, the stuff I was thinking about was wrong. I was thinking, dreaming really, about my son growing up to be this stellar athlete, a kid filled with confidence, who had big dreams built into him at birth and was destined to live them out. I was also thinking about making sure that I was a good father, doing all I could to earn and pay for the great life that awaited him."

I stopped myself for a moment, asking Marlene to pass the tissues.

Gathering myself, I continued, "When Gavin's very existence was in question, my thoughts, my perspective changed 180 degrees. Instead of imagining out-of-town hockey tournaments where my kid scores the overtime goal and envisioning him making a speech to his high school classmates as valedictorian, I thought about holding him and seeing him laugh and watching him fall asleep on Patty. When life forced me to change my perspective, it opened a world to my new eyes.

"I must tell you that the day Gavin left NICU and came home, I walked into the house a changed person. A better person, I believe. Just like you promised Curtis, I too promised something. I made the promise to myself that when life was telling me to grow, in this case, to change how I looked at things, I would recognize it and I would do it. At this moment in your life, I feel like it's fair to say your retirement plan needs a different perspective so that you may be opened up to see things with fresh eyes."

Marlene played with her coffee cup. I observed her looking out in every direction before settling on a random spot on the conference room table.

"Let's do it," she said, finally raising her gaze.

We rolled up our sleeves. The time went fast. We exhausted the minutes in collaboration. I asked lots of questions about her goals, her dreams, her ideal life. Marlene answered each of them. We discussed options. She asked questions back, me answering each of them.

The process was becoming a forum of transformation, which would later serve as the bedrock of empowerment for moving forward in her retirement.

"In the past," I said, "you had financial advisors who talked mostly about making your money grow. 'Appreciation' was probably the buzzword. Sound about right?"

"Exactly right," responded Marlene. "I heard the same things from both Curtis' advisor and the one my son-in-law recommended. Whether it was when the principal was at its all-time high or when the value was going down, they talked about growth until they were blue in the face."

Which is why we changed the perspective. We were switching the focus of her portfolio from one kind of ROI to another ROI.

My pencil tip rested on the pie chart in front of us. I had broken down the slices comprising Marlene's portfolio. Below the chart, I'd put a large circle around three words, written in huge bold letters.

"Reliability of Income," she read aloud.

"That's right," I said, "not Return on Investment, but Reliability of Income. It summarizes the plan we're designing for you. This is going to be the focus of your 'Estate Recovery Plan.'

"From what you've told me, between Social Security and your pension, you have enough income to pay your bills and do all the things you enjoy. Trips. Christmas presents. Helping to pay for camps, athletics, whatever, for your grandchildren. The 'Estate Recovery Plan' is about protecting your portfolio and instituting a framework for modest, if any, gains, in which your principal doesn't risk losing value while still allowing you to draw income by way of planned, calculated draws."

IF YOU HAVE INVESTED FOR A LONG WHILE NOW, YOU PROBABLY KNOW THE DIFFERENCE BETWEEN CONSERVATIVE, MODERATE, AND AGGRESSIVE INVESTING. YOU MIGHT HAVE EVEN ADOPTED AN AGGRESSIVE INVESTING PLAN IN THE PAST. BUT IN RETIREMENT, IT'S ALMOST NEVER A GOOD IDEA TO PUT THE MONEY YOU NEED FOR INCOME INTO HIGH-RISK INVESTMENTS. IF YOUR FINANCIAL ADVISOR IS TELLING YOU TO ENTER INTO RISKY INVESTMENTS AT RETIREMENT AGE, THIS MIGHT BE A SIGN TO LOOK FOR SOMEONE ELSE.

By creating a plan that's built to protect and safeguard the nest egg, I added, further peace of mind is built in, just in case, should Marlene require assisted living care or residence in a nursing home someday.

"God willing, you will never need that type of care," I told her. "But if you do, this money is there to cover it. If you shouldn't, well, then you'll have that inheritance to pass along."

Marlene finished her coffee with one last healthy swig. She reclined in her chair oh-so-slightly and her eyes cast out the window, gazing toward the powder-blue sky.

"I was in ruins when I arrived here today," Marlene said. "On top of the broken heart I've had ever since Curtis' passing, my anxieties and fears have been compounding over time because of this uncertain retirement piece. For the first time in a long, long time, I feel as if I have some control. The feeling this gives me at this very moment—"

Marlene's voice trailed off. I smiled, trying to convey my feelings without words.

We finished the session by adding a final component to Marlene's Estate Recovery Plan, arranging for her to purchase a life insurance plan that will pay out 80 percent of the nest egg principal that had been lost.

Marlene began to cry once more. Not tears of sorrow. They didn't originate from a place of fear.

"Look at me," she said, laughing at herself. "I can't stop crying today."

Her countenance said so much. It brought me joy.

"Today, by listening, explaining, caring," she said, "you showed me something, Joe. You communicated with me in such a way that revealed the kind of person you are, the type of professional helpfulness you provide, the kind of company you have here. Today, you have given me a gift I will not soon forget."

CHAPTER 5

"Be Better Than You Are"

I've got a confession to make. I still feel a healthy dose of wonder every time my son calls me "Dad."

My wife Patty and I welcomed Gavin into the world with tears of gratitude a decade ago. With the dangers of his premature birth in the rearview, he began to walk in no time at all. Yet today, like yesterday, and every time before, whenever Gavin says, "Dad," my insides turn into gooey caramel sauce.

Now, it's a struggle for me to remember what life was like before fatherhood. It might be sappy or cliché, but I know my life began anew the day I first held Gavin. I hold onto the memory of that moment as if it was as essential to living as breathing.

The same can be said for the day Gavin first sounded out the word: "Dad." The moment lives inside me as if it happened yesterday.

The carpeted living room floor served as the setting. There was stink in the air. With Patty gone on a business trip, I was on solo parent duty, dealing with a diaper hazmat situation with a dangerously low supply of wipes. But the dire situation would dissipate, with the sweetest two-beat of sounds.

"Da'da," Gavin said.

Had he just said what I thought I heard him say?

"Da'da," he repeated.

I almost fell over. My body flushed with pride, duty, love. So there we were. Parked on the floor. Gavin bare bummed. Me marinated in tears. Team Gavin-and-Dad was smiling like we'd discovered the meaning of life.

Maybe we had.

Gavin was too small to remember the moment. I know that. For Dad, though, I continue to find myself irregularly asking him if he does, hoping if I ask enough times, it will become a shared moment between the two of us. But that's not to say the Gavin-and-Dad Dream Team hasn't been on fire making memories.

I want to share one with you. It's my hope that it helps you get a better sense of who I am, this person who is many things. A son who is equal parts proud and humble. A patriot. A loving, yet imperfect husband. Dad. A CERTIFIED FINANCIAL PLANNER™ professional. A small business owner and employer. A military veteran.

The seeds for the memory were sowed in happenstance. Gavin hadn't yet turned eight years old. It was Sunday, the Sunday in March after the end of the Minnesota State High School Hockey Tournament.

Gavin and Dad were bummed out, to say the least.

The annual tournament is the sports pinnacle of our calendar. Gavin already eyes playing in it. He's a right-winger who doesn't mind crashing the net. His skating needs work. He still doesn't use enough deep knee-bend despite the countless times I've reminded him that's what makes Sidney Crosby *Sidney Crosby*. Which also serves as a reminder to me that I'm Dad, not coach.

The game didn't go too well. The mood of game night spilled over into the next day.

Patty was out of the house volunteering at church. The two of us had eaten lunch. With last night's high school hockey title game in the record books, both of us felt deflated. Outside, dirty overcast skies and wind chills, compliments of the Snow Miser, added to a downer mood. With no high school hockey to look forward to and not one semi-decent sporting event on television, I'd decided to search for a movie we both could enjoy.

As coincidence would have it, the movie "Miracle" was just starting. It's the story of the U.S. men's hockey team that defeated the Soviets en route to winning the gold medal at the 1980 Winter Olympics in Lake Placid.

Gavin knew bits and pieces of the story, but, as Dad, I knew my son had yet to understand how epic the storyline actually was.

During the opening minutes, I observed Gavin, curious to see how he would receive the movie. The look on his face gave me the answer. Men in yucky brown suits and feathered hair, hockey players in practically medieval gear playing with Northland sticks. It just wasn't the stuff for his cinematic hockey wheelhouse.

"Give it until the fifteen-minute mark," I told him. "I'll keep time. So if you think it's still a dog in six minutes and seventeen seconds, sixteen, fifteen, we can see if there's something else on."

Gavin begrudgingly agreed.

"Trust me on this. If there's two things I know, it's I love you as much as any dad has ever loved his kid, and secondly, "Miracle" is a great, I mean a great, movie. Watch and you will know about the greatest hockey story, ever."

For the next two hours, my son was transfixed. In Kurt Russell's portrayal of hockey legend and U.S. Head Coach Herb Brooks, Gavin witnessed the traits of what it means to live life as a rugged humanitarian. Respect. Humility. Grit. Passion. Dedication. Love. Truth.

There is a scene that would prove unforgettable in my son's mind. It's the scene in which Brooks barks at his players during practice, saying, "The legs feed the wolf."

"The legs feed the wolf."

Not long after that viewing, I learned how much Gavin loved that saying. It was in the morning. I was almost out the house door, headed for the office.

"Have a good day, Dad," said Gavin. "Work hard. I know you will. And don't forget: The legs feed the wolf."

The day Gavin-and-Dad first watched "Miracle" together four years ago began a tradition. With every first Sunday in March following the state tournament comes the memory anew.

Gavin-and-Dad find our seats. We'll spend two hours-plus hours absorbing "Miracle" again. It's become an annual event we created together. What started as a movie shared one Sunday years ago will forever be a gift from Gavin to Dad.

He'll understand what I mean on the day he's supposed to. He'll get it the day he hears himself being called Dad for the first time, although it might not be in two syllables.

Like Gavin, I too have a favorite Herb Brooks' saying. It consists of thirty words he told his players during their ascent into history.

"Let me start with issuing you a challenge: Be better than you are," said Brooks. "Set a goal that seems unattainable, and when you reach that goal, set another one even higher."

I founded Secured Retirement Financial to give people who've given their best as spouses, parents and workers, the most comprehensive retirement planning experience available.

Founding the company on the highest principles of humanity, I challenged myself to create a framework from which retirement planning is no longer overwhelming and incomplete, but personal, empowering, and all encompassing.

At Secured Retirement Financial, we don't serve clients. We serve people. We build and serve relationships, relationships built with trust, candor, integrity, and respect.

People entrust Secured Retirement Financial with their lives and dreams. For that, my staff and myself are honored. Our pledge is to cherish, protect, and honor your trust.

This is done the very same way that I hold on to the memory of the moment I was changing a diaper and listened to my son turn a four-letter word into two syllables of auditory gold.

I do believe Gavin-and-Dad were taught the meaning of life that day: To live in the moment. Every moment.

I can't think of a better way.

CHAPTER 6

Excellence Awaits You

Reflect back for a moment. Into time. Into your personal history.

Of course, you look fabulous. And almost always thinner than you thought you were—funny how that works. Besides that, what do you see? Maybe the bachelor apartment in a dicey part of the city. Perhaps the moment you met the person who would become your spouse. Maybe the heinous carpet in the office where your career started.

Life has a way of changing each and every one of us. Along with a career, wedding vows, and family, a day arrived when somebody said you needed a financial advisor. Heeding the advice, you went out and found yourself one.

The person may have been a friend from college who worked in the sector. The advisor, with an ironclad reputation of investing in stocks, mutual funds, and IRAs, might have come on your radar screen from a friend of a neighbor whose aunt knew somebody referring you to said person in a glass and steel office tower in Bloomington, Woodbury, or downtown Minneapolis.

So it began.

Your advisor recommended certain financial products. They were described in terms of handsome appreciation, maybe risk.

They talked. You listened. You said okay, instructing your advisor to pull the trigger on whatever buy or sell it happened to be. In fulfilling the task, the advisor pocketed a commission. This was the nature of the acquaintanceship because you couldn't truly call it a relationship. It was financial advising and client investing based on a transactional level of service.

Quarterly statements arrived by mail. What was revealed inside the envelopes elicited good vibrations or unnerving displeasures.

If it was the latter, you called your advisor or paid them a visit. The advisor might have suggested another product that looked promising or opined how your portfolio needed new blood.

Maybe you were one of the lucky ones. Perhaps you owned a beefy enough portfolio that your advisor delivered a more intimate level of service.

If that was the case, they talked to you that time you were pondering staying at a rental townhouse versus purchasing your first home. The advisor reached out to you one day and said it was time for term life insurance. They offered counsel about starting a college fund for your newborn. Maybe they went through the same spiel when a second child arrived. And the third.

So here you are. At this moment. Discovering Secured Retirement Financial. Maybe for the first time.

We're glad you're here.

At this very moment, I can tell you that you're standing at a new threshold. With established families and well-healed careers approaching their autumn, up ahead is a golden-rimmed horizon. In the not-so-distant future, retirement awaits.

Are you prepared? Is your retirement planning all that it should be?

Your IRA might have grown to an amount worth more than you ever envisioned. Camping trips to the Boundary Waters in lieu of airfare and hotel to Disney World, and bag lunches instead of restaurant fare during the workweek; these small sacrifices paid off. The kids have left the house. Your mortgage is almost gone, or perhaps it was paid off a few years back.

With all signs telling you that you've got matters under control, you can't help but bask in the thought that you're floating into retirement. Because you did all the right things, saving, working hard, contending for world's best parents year-in and year-out, in your heart of hearts, there's the belief your retirement plan is airtight, rock solid.

So it should be.

But reality can turn harsh in a finger snap. Even in retirement, especially for retirees. Unfortunately, it's a lesson too many learn after it's too late.

It happens with the discovery that retirement plans can have holes. In some cases, the holes were so big, so overlooked, the golden years derailed due to circumstances that weren't addressed in the planning process.

The number one reason this happens is because a retirement plan wasn't much of a plan after all.

Secured Retirement Financial was created because retirees and those soon-to-be retired deserve a level of service excellence.

Invest a little of your time today and it can return a retirement planning experience. Invest some of your time now and Secured Retirement Financial will show you our process that's comprehensive, interconnected, personal, engaged. In our process is your partnership.

It's a level of service that I believe is unequaled in the financial services industry. It's why I started Secured Retirement Financial twenty-three years ago, a company that operates from a philosophy in living.

It's doing things the only way, the right way. It's treating people right, which means, with Secured Retirement Financial, you'll have a relationship built for life, not just an advisor for a season. It's eye contact, handshakes that mean something, and true listening. It's the process of building the retirement plan that's right for each person, every couple.

My name is Joe Lucey. As Secured Retired Financial founder and president, I'm excited to collaborate with you, earn your trust, and create the retirement plan that helps to insure the golden years shine beyond your expectations.

Secured Retirement Financial's engaged level of retirement planning service is understanding who you are, not as a client, but as a well-rounded human being who is more than your bank account, more than your job, more than your family role. We want to learn your financial goals and create an in-depth knowledge of what you want your life to look like come retirement.

We'll be asking lots of questions. We'll be listening even more. We do this so that your custom-made retirement plan is comprehensive, all-encompassing to a fault, streamlined at receiving and spending income in the most tax-efficient ways possible and prepared for every conceivable scenario so that everything is accounted for and well prepared.

An engaged level of service means people. Our staff consists of experts who will collaborate with you using the Secured Retirement Blueprint™. Together, we will design an income plan anchored by Social Security and tax efficiency. At Secured Retirement Financial, "engaged" means an EKG stress test of your investment portfolio, in which the overall health and volatility of your personal retirement savings, will be measured against your retirement goals one year removed, five years from now, and to retirement infinity and beyond (well, not quite that far, but you get the point).

An engaged level of service is planning for healthcare costs, establishing a framework if a spouse should get sick, requiring extended, sometimes indefinite time in a nursing facility, and planning for the time when one spouse predeceases the other.

At Secured Retirement Financial, I make my pledge to you. I am a son, husband, and father. And as a small business owner, I can promise you that myself, my team, and this company is dedicated to delivering nothing less than your best retirement plan possible.

You sacrificed and worked hard to get here. You deserve the retirement you dream about. You deserve the retirement planning service excellence of Secured Retirement Financial.

Let's get started, shall we?

About the Author

Joseph S. Lucey is a CERTIFIED FINANCIAL PLANNER™ professional and Registered Financial Consultant who leads a team of advisors as president of Minneapolis-based Secured Retirement Financial. With nearly twenty-five years of experience in the financial services arena, his Secured Retirement Blueprint™ process has helped several thousand families achieve a secure and independent retirement through comprehensive financial planning.

He is a frequent contributor in various media forums, among them hosting the weekly "Secured Retirement Radio" program that airs on TwinCities Newstalk AM1130 on Saturday mornings. He is a nationally recognized "RetireMentor" for Dow Jones-owned MarketWatch online. He is a frequent contributing author on retirement planning issues with insights and strategies geared to the objectives, concerns, risks, and opportunities facing retirees and those transitioning into retirement. He also is a member of the Ed Slott Master Elite IRA Advisor Group.

Outside of work, he enjoys spending time with his wife, Patty, and son, Gavin, who shares his father's love of hockey. He and his family are active in their church and community through projects such as Make-A-Wish, Second Harvest, Fisher House, and the Minnesota Military Family Foundation. He is an active supporter of youth hockey and a season-ticket holder of the NHL's Minnesota Wild.

About Secured Retirement Financial

Planning for retirement isn't about one thing, or achieving some "magical" number.

It's about many things working together.

It's about minimizing your taxes, so you keep more of your hard-earned money in your pocket.

It's about turning your savings and investments into an income workhorse, while minimizing your risk.

It's about wringing every nickel out of your Social Security benefits.

It's about protecting you from the skyrocketing cost of health care, and long-term care.

And it's about creating a strategy for inflation, protecting your estate, and so much more.

At Secured Retirement Financial, we take a team approach to help you tackle all these issues. And when everything works together, it can have a profound impact on making your money go a lot further in retirement.

No two financial plans are alike. And your plan will be totally unique to you, and your specific needs. Because even a minor difference in age, assets, risk tolerance, or longevity could trigger a major shift in strategy.

With financial professionals on staff that bring decades of experience helping people like you prepare for and execute financial strategies specifically designed for retirement income, our team works diligently for our clients. The stories in this book reflect the experiences we try to foster.

Retirement is a once-in-a-lifetime experience for most of us, one that will hopefully last for decades. We believe the comprehensive approach to financial planning we take at Secured Retirement Financial will ultimately help you make the most out of every dollar you've saved for retirement.

Contact

While I wrote this book to illustrate what an experience at Secured Retirement Financial might look like, it is by no means an exhaustive look at every financial option that might be right for you. If you have more questions and would like to work with a financial professional who can give you a more comprehensive overview of your finances, give me a call. Whether you are a fit to work with me or whether you might benefit from a referral, I'm here to help:

Joe Lucey
Secured Retirement Financial
www.securedretirements.com
Phone: (952) 460-3260 | Fax: (952) 460-3261
info@securedretirements.com

5775 Wayzata Blvd, Ste 830
St. Louis Park, MN 55416